10 STEPS TO Z-Z-ZING!

Exodus 20:1–17
for children

Written by Joan E. Curren

Illustrated by Bill Heuer

CONCORDIA PUBLISHING HOUSE · SAINT LOUIS

God's people were slaves in Egypt.
Their masters were so wrong
To hurt them, but God heard them pray.
He sent a leader strong.

Then Moses warned their masters cruel
Of plagues with frogs and flies,
Of hailstorms, locusts, others too.
The land was filled with cries

Of "Let them go!" "Get out of here!"
"Our pride your God destroys!"
So out of Egypt Moses led
Men, women, girls, and boys.

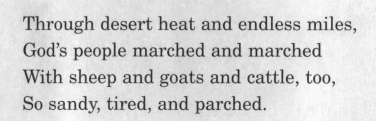

Through desert heat and endless miles,
God's people marched and marched
With sheep and goats and cattle, too,
So sandy, tired, and parched.

And how they whined! At Moses raged!
`Til God said, "Moses climb
Mount Sinai, and Ten Rules I'll give—
Ten Steps to guide your time.

"I brought you out from Egyptland
And bonds of slavery.
The First Step is: *You worship not
Another God but Me*.

"You must not worship
Any gods or idols before Me,
Not any shape of anything
In heaven, earth, or sea.

"The Second Step: *Don't use My name*
To curse or tell a lie,
But use it only prayerfully,
My name to glorify.

"Step Number Three I give to you:
Don't work on Sabbath days.
They're holy, and they're made for rest
And time to give Me praise.

"Here's Number Four! It's next in line.
Your Dad and Mom obey.
And in this way you honor them,
Show love for them each day.

"*Do not kill* is Number Five,
For killing contradicts
My love for all created life.
Next comes Number Six.

"*Don't take another person's spouse.*
That's called *adultery*.
A husband and a wife belong
Together and to Me.

"Number Seven says: *Don't steal*.
It means don't be a thief
Who takes things that another owns
For it will bring you grief.

"Now, Number Eight is *Do not lie*
At any time of day.
Speak only truth and you'll show love
For Me by what you say.

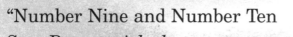

"Number Nine and Number Ten
Say: *Do not wish that you
Could have the things your neighbor owns.
His joy should be yours, too.*"

God gave these rules to be obeyed,
Ten Steps for following.
Although we fail we know God's saving grace
Gives our life Z-Z-Zing!"

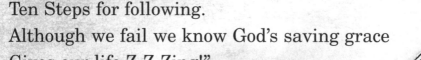

Dear Parents:

The Ten Commandments given to Moses and God's people are just as relevant for us today. They help us know when we sin and serve to keep order in our world. They also function as a guide to help us, as Christians, know what we should and should not do to lead a God-pleasing life.

God desires that we keep His commandments perfectly, but we all fall short because of our sinful nature. As you teach these commandments to your children, remind them that God sent Jesus to take the punishment for all the times we sin and do not keep His commandments. This is the message of the Gospel. Eternal life in heaven is waiting for all who believe in the saving power of the death and resurrection of Jesus.

Join together as a family to find as many things as possible that come in groups of ten. Remind each other that the commandments come in tens too. Pray that, by the power of the Holy Spirit, you might follow these Ten Steps and experience the *Z-Z-ZING* of God's grace and forgiveness in your lives.

The Editor